Artwork © Darrel Morris
Author: Ann Wiens
Series Editor: Matthew Koumis
Graphic Design: Rachael Dadd
Reprographics: Ermanno Beverari
Printed in Italy by Grafiche AZ

© Telos Art Publishing 2003
Telos Art Publishing
PO Box 125, Winchester
SO23 7UJ England
T   +44 (0) 1962 864546
F   +44 (0) 1962 864727
E   editorial@telos.net
E   sales@telos.net
W www.arttextiles.com

ISBN 1 902015 69 X (softback)

A CIP catalogue record for this book
is available from The British Library.

Notes
All dimensions are shown in imperial
and metric, height x width x depth.

Photo Credits
BLACK/TOBY photography, Amy
Honchell

Artist's Acknowledgments
I am grateful to Amy Honchell,
Lindsay Packer, and Rebecca
Ringquist for all their support in my
studio. I wish to thank Brenda Black,
Susie Brandt, Leroy Moore, Daniel
Scarangella and Lewis Toby for their
encouragement and patience,
especially in the dark times.

Thanks to Alison Ferris and Ann
Wiens for their generous, insightful,
talented writing.

Publisher's Acknowledgments
Thanks to Paul Richardson of Oxford
Brookes University; also to Leo
Pickford, John Denison, Freya,
Alessandra, Simone, Marco, Moreno,
and the gnocchi chef at Nella's.

illustration on pages 1 & 48
Climb
2002
thread, canvas
6.5 x 6.5ft (2 x 2m)

front cover illustration:
Pointing (detail)
2002
thread, canvas
4.8 x 6.3ft (1.5 x 2m)

back cover illustration:
Playing Right Field
1990
found fabric, sewing thread, canvas
6.5 x 7in (17 x 18cm)

12-50

South East Essex College
of Arts and Technology Southend

portfolio collection
Darrel Morris

TELOS

Contents

Allowed to Open the Door
1992
found fabric, sewing thread, canvas
9 x 6in (23.4 x 15.6cm)

Foreword

Darrel Morris's poignant miniature needleworks pack a punch. Using cast-off cloth upon which he appliqués and embroiders, Morris addresses masculinity from a queer perspective and, by extension, comes to grip with matters such as shame and humiliation, melancholy and mourning, and the abuse of power as they are experienced every day. Despite the somber topics, however, Morris's elaborately and colorfully embroidered images of men and boys – rendered like characters in comic strips – result in powerful and humorous, if often forlorn, narratives.

It is impossible not to read Morris's work, at least in part, as autobiographical. Morris comes from Appalachia – specifically southeastern Kentucky – which remains the United States' unacknowledged Third World. Most Americans know little about the complicated social, cultural, economic, and political histories of the region, not to mention its current catastrophic environmental conditions. Instead, movies such as *Deliverance* – which contains perhaps the most degrading stereotypes of Appalachia – have informed most Americans. Morris does not address the politics of this region directly, but they are, I think, intrinsically incorporated into his work. For instance, Morris's work persistently explores the ramifications of all kinds of disempowerment – from economic to psychological – which are certainly related to the politics of Appalachia, as well as to his experiences of growing up there as a queer kid. But the most obvious and most important way Morris's work refers to the region is in his use of textiles.

Along with basket making and all sorts of woodworking (the production of everything from furniture to musical instruments), Appalachia has a rich textile tradition. When hand-craft traditions were superseded by the Industrial Revolution in the United States, Northern missionaries in the late nineteenth century reveled in the fact that the isolated mountain regions appeared untouched by these technological advancements and that the making of hand-made objects still proliferated. These missionaries set out to preserve the traditions, arguing that it provided cultural identity as well as a means of economic support for the isolated and impoverished mountain people who survived primarily on subsistence farming as well as by raising tobacco and working in coal mines. Textile production – namely quilt-making and weaving – was deemed, by then, a primarily female occupation and it succeeded in providing a sense of pride and community for its participants. Morris's use of textiles is in this respect especially pointed: instead of employing them in a celebratory manner, he uses them to express feelings of shame and alienation especially in regards to failing to meet the local standards of masculinity –

a failure that includes, of course, the choice to pursue art making. But Morris's strategy is more complicated and layered than a simple reversal of opposites such as pride and shame or community and alienation – and that is where country music comes in.

Unlike popular films about the region, country music has portrayed a more nuanced, complex and human Appalachia to the rest of the world and Morris acknowledges that there is a bit of country music in his work. For instance, his works, like country music, are narratives that contain raw expressions of heartbreak and longing, as well as a self-deprecating sense of humor. But the kind of country music that resonates in Morris's work is not the slickly packaged macho honky-tonk or self-pitying crooning you hear on AM radio stations. It is, instead, the kind you'd hear today in Chicago clubs. Alternative country music – known

by many as insurgent country – retains the emotional intensity but abstains from the corporatized melodrama of mainstream country and sometimes incorporates a bit of punk-rock unruliness while at the same time staying faithful to the traditions. Like the contemporary musicians who embrace the tradition of country music but resist or alter particular aspects of it, Morris self-consciously chooses to pursue "crafts" and picks through its complex social and cultural history to fuel the power and meaning of his work.

Morris's decision to involve his art in the traditions of hand-made textiles today is one that risks going unnoticed in a world that continues to be – often unquestioningly – seduced by technology. Those who just as quickly reject technology and idealize – and depoliticize – the hand-made (much like the nineteenth-century missionaries) will not find solace in Morris's work.

THE MOMENT I REALIZED I WASN'T THAT GREAT OF AN ARTIST.

Darrel Morris's work offers us a more thoughtful and more satisfying vision of where we are now: propelled ever forward into an uncertain future but inextricably tied to a past that continues to move us, even if not to consolation.

Alison Ferris
Curator
Bowdoin College Museum of Art

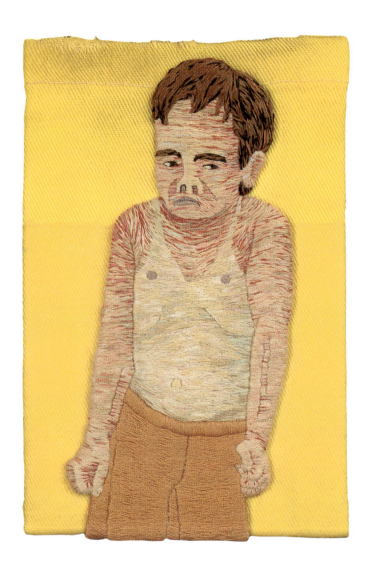

page 7:
The Moment
1992
found fabric, thread, canvas
8 x 10in (21 x 26cm)
Collection of Loyola University,
Chicago, Department of Fine Arts

left:
Mad Baby
1990
found fabric, sewing thread,
acrylic medium, canvas
6 x 4in (16 x 10.5cm)

Darrel Morris

by Ann Wiens

I'm Nobody! Who are you?
Are you – Nobody – Too?
Then there's a pair of us?
Don't tell! They'd advertise – you know!

How dreary – to be – Somebody!
How public – like a Frog –
To tell one's name – the livelong June –
To an admiring Bog!
Emily Dickinson

Laughter is serious. More complicated,
more serious than tears.
Toni Morrison

The man is the one we see first. He is an archetype of paternal authority gone bad, his body taut as a spring, one hand clenched in a fist, the other pointing, furiously jabbing at the air as he stomps his foot and yells. Even his necktie writhes in anger or frustration. He fills the doorframe in which he stands, his tense form bulging slightly off the surface of the embroidered image that contains him. He is somebody making himself heard, shouting, stamping, gesticulating. In the context of this tiny, obsessively stitched vignette of domestic dysfunction, at least, he is somebody with power.

The man is the one we see first. But the object of his rage is where our attention lingers. In the lower right corner of the picture is the image of a little boy, sitting with his back to us. He is transparent, rendered with just a simple thread outline stitched into the deep brown fabric of the floor. Although we can't see his face, he appears startled, abruptly interrupted as he quietly draws a picture on a sheet of notebook paper: a childish, pointy-roofed house. He is nobody; small, voiceless, faceless, powerless against the tumble of angry words the man hurls toward him across the picture: *NEVER USE GOOD PAPER TO DRAW ON! USE THE BACK OF A CALENDAR OR THE INSIDE OF AN OLD ENVELOPE.*

He is nobody; even the illicit sheet of 'good' paper is more emphatically rendered than he is.

left:
Good Paper (detail)
thread, canvas
8 x 6.5in (21 x 17cm)

page 12:
Interview
1993
embroidery and appliqué
5 x 12in (13 x 31cm)

As discomfiting as this image is, it is also laced with humor. The awkward, cartoonish contortions of the father; the incongruously tranquil, leaf-patterned blue fabric that makes up the walls; the father's ridiculous overreaction to such an innocuous transgression; even the notion that anyone saw fit to painstakingly embroider this scene – not sketch it, not paint it, but embroider it in dense satin stitch with sewing thread – all lend it a certain dark funniness born of incredulity and discomfort. It seems so straightforward at first; a narrative of a painful childhood moment, recalled and depicted with cartoon-like directness, right down to the word balloon. But it is so much more complicated than that.

The work is *Good Paper*, an 8 by 6 inches image in embroidery and appliqué by Chicago-based artist Darrel Morris. It depicts a confrontation Morris remembers from when the artist was four or five years old. It began with a drawing of the father alone, and finally found completion ten years later, when Morris struck upon the idea of making the little boy transparent – barely there, nobody. The embroidery is done with sewing thread, not embroidery floss; the appliqué incorporates fabric from an old pair of the artist's pants and a much-worn sweatshirt his mother once gave him for Christmas. Like so much of Morris's work, it is sad and funny; awkward and beautiful; simple and obsessive; comfortingly familiar and disturbingly odd. The narrative is clear, the story it tells poignant. The materials – soft fabric, old, worn clothes, thread – are tactile and familiar. The evocation of labor is exhausting – the trace of the artist's hand, the evidence of endless hours spent with needle and thread. The combination is extraordinary. In a world where might makes right and history is written by the winners, Morris tells the stories of the nobodies, of those who – because they are young, or poor, or meek, or quiet, or scared – are systematically disenfranchised. Within the closed societies of the family, the school, or the office, this everyday oppression is largely accepted. In these intimate, colorful panels of worn fabric and sewing thread, Morris makes it clear – without sourness or sentimentality – just how unacceptable these everyday inequities really are.

What's the world for if you can't make it up the way you want it?
Toni Morrison

Darrel Morris grew up on the outskirts of Barbourville, Kentucky, a little coal-mining town nestled within the western fringes of the Appalachian Mountains. It is the seat of Knox County, in the middle of an area known as the Eastern Kentucky coal field; a hilly, rural place of dense hardwood forests slashed through with abandoned coal shafts and

once-lush mountains laid bare by decades of strip mining. Nearly 40 percent of the county live below the poverty line; half are considered functionally illiterate; 38 percent never finished high school. Coal mining is still the county's primary industry. Morris was raised in a fundamentalist Southern Baptist household, where gender roles were sharply delineated and anything that looked more like play than work was considered somewhat immoral. His father, a coal miner, suffered from undiagnosed clinical depression and was often abusive. There were no other children Morris's age nearby to play with and he was often alone, his physical isolation compounded by extreme shyness. He lived with the fear that he would be trapped in this bleak community, a miner like his father, his

uncles, his neighbors. But he found an escape, a temporary refuge, next door in the home of his grandmother, Pearl.

Pearl Morris was a great storyteller and craftsperson. Darrel would spend hours with her, braiding rags that she would fashion into rugs, learning to quilt and sew, listening to the stories she would tell as they worked. At her side, he and his sister learned traditional Appalachian crafts – Dianne Simpson now makes her living as a weaver and basket-maker in Kentucky – as well all the popular craft projects of the time: candle making, découpage, macramé. It was an escape, something to occupy the time of a lonely boy, but it also offered a powerful counterbalance to the bleakness and negativity that surrounded him. It was here that

Morris learned the positive value – spiritual as well as practical – of creativity, of adding a bit of beauty to the world, of making something from nothing.

There are many, many reasons artists make art. But among the most compelling is the desire to make a better world than the one they're experiencing. As he neared adulthood, Morris began thinking more and more about how to do just that. Listening to politically informed folk music of the time – Bob Dylan, Joni Mitchell, Carole King – and watching the violent, year-long 1973 mine-workers' strike unfold in nearby Harlan County, provided models of people voicing their objection to an inequitable world, changing it in small but inspiring ways.

A few years later, Morris's 'big break' came as a one-two punch involving unemployment and a car accident. Fired from his job running the gun and automotive section of a TG&Y discount store, and with insurance money from the accident, Morris unexpectedly found himself with both the time and the resources to go to college. He enrolled in Eastern Kentucky University in Richmond, an 80-mile leap away from Barbourville. There he earned a two-year associate's degree in drafting and engineering design, and got a job as a draftsman at IBM. He enjoyed drafting – one of his first assignments involved taking apart an electric typewriter and meticulously drawing each of its individual parts – but he hated the job. He hated the corporate culture, the power structure, the 'hunting and fishing' office camaraderie of which he was not a part, and the expectation that being a draftsman was merely a step on the ladder toward becoming an engineer, a ladder he had no interest in climbing.

In Morris's images of the workaday world, the imbalance of power addressed in so many of his images of children is shifted to the context of the workplace. In these inequitable power plays, we recognize – and perhaps relive – the sting of rejection, the shame of powerlessness, the degradation inherent in the corporate structure. In *Interview* for example, a tiny man sits in a hard, wooden chair so large that his feet dangle well above the floor. He faces a massive desk, behind which reclines a much larger figure in white shirt and tie. A long, thin, word balloon stretches threateningly toward the smaller man, dismissing his existence with the words *YOU'RE NOT EXACTLY WHAT WE HAD IN MIND*.

In *Company Picnic*, three slightly paunchy, middle-aged men in shirts and ties join in an embarrassing act of forced congeniality: a hula-hoop contest. They are thickly embroidered in varying degrees of detail; the uncooperative hoop of the foremost figure cutting a striking red line through the scrap of avocado-green towel that serves as grass.

above:

Daddy

2001

found fabric, sewing thread, canvas

10 x 8in (26 x 21cm)

Collection of Christopher E. Vroom
and Illya Szilak

page 13:

Company picnic (detail)

1997

found fabric, sewing thread, canvas

7 x 7in (18 x 18cm)

Collection of Lorraine
and Harold Paddor

The piece is lighter in mood than many of Morris's images; the thought of these grown men gyrating in their shirts and ties is undeniably funny. But the humor is complex; it has a cruel bite to it. It seems probable that these men are willing to suspend their personal dignity, to make fools of themselves in a desperate attempt to show they're good sports, team players, value-adding employees who exceed expectations and should move up a rung on the corporate ladder – or at least avoid sliding down.

At IBM, Morris produced mechanical drawings of typewriter parts from nine to five; after work, he taught himself to paint. Within a year, his apartment was full of paintings, and he found himself asking questions about color theory and art history that his 'how-to' books were not prepared to answer. So he enrolled in the Fine Arts Department at the University of Kentucky in Lexington (there were now about 100 miles between him and

Barbourville), borrowing the money to get through. The 2001 piece *Daddy* recalls this period, when Morris asked his father for the money to take the college-entrance exams. Sprawled on an off-kilter green kitchen chair, the now-aging father figure scoffs: *COLLEGE – YOU'RE NO BETTER TO WORK FOR A LIVING THAN I AM.*

Driven by a sense of desperate urgency fueled by a combination of his family's lack of faith, his increasing debt, a fundamentalist-tinged work ethic, and the need to know everything as quickly as possible, he never missed a class. He had his own studio, and stayed there late every night, working. He would complete all his course requirements within the first month, then concentrate on his own work the rest of the term, trying everything that occurred to him. By the time he graduated, his work had been included in half a dozen professional exhibitions.

Morris moved to Chicago in 1985, drawn by the city's demonstrated love of folk and outsider art, and by the reputation of The School of the Art Institute of Chicago's Department of Fiber and Material Studies, a progressive department that placed as much importance on the conceptual aspects of fiber and textile arts as it did on the technical and historical. It was here, immersed in the study of global textile histories while at the same time exposed to the buzz of the city and the immediacy of the contemporary art world, that Morris refined his art, deftly interweaving these influences into the work for which he has become known.

Morris's work is often shown in the context of painting, and his experience as a painter and appreciation for the history of painting are apparent in the embroideries. He cites artists such as Frida Kahlo and George Grosz as influences, both for their biting cultural commentary and the beauty of their work. An interest in the broader emotional impact and experiential effect of color field painting is evident in his abstracted backgrounds, and especially in his more recent, large-scale monochromatic works. Morris still does occasional paintings for fun, or to work out color issues in preparation for the more labor-intensive embroideries. And interestingly, nearly all the embroideries are based on preliminary collages, many featuring newspaper images that Morris has collected for years – he has thousands, organized by category. The 1988 collage *Mid Management*, for example, depicts four men making gestures of measurement – one figure leans into the picture from the right, his barely separated finger and thumb indicating 'teensy weensy'; others make more-or-less 'fish-size' gestures, holding their hands shoulder-width apart or so. The image is a particularly funny one, but again has a bite to it, pointing up what Morris sees as a peculiarly male urge to measure everything. Like many of the collages, this led eventually to an embroidery, *Mid Management* of 1993. Nearly all Morris's images come from found sources, primarily newspaper photos. He feels this quotation lends them a certain authority, but it also imbues them with edginess, a compelling awkwardness that comes partly from the imperfect melding of disparate images from various sources. The most complex works, however, have to eventually become embroideries; for much of their power is derived from their materiality. And Morris's

choice of material is never random; each scrap of fabric has a history and a reason for inclusion. These images are embroidered with sewing thread, not embroidery floss, partly for the added tension the thread-thin line creates, but also for the hugely expanded color options. As available thread colors necessarily follow the fashions of the times, Morris maintains a collection of 'vintage' thread in discontinued colors, the difference between, say, a 1973 orange and a 2003 orange being significant in evoking the appropriate era in an image. Likewise, much of the background and appliqué fabric is taken from old clothing, either the artist's or pieces found in thrift stores. The worn, outdated fabric of clothing, blankets, and the like lends these images a visual and emotional depth that new, fabric-store material could never achieve.

page 15:
Mid Management
1988
collage, acrylic, ink
8.5 x 11in (21 x 28.5cm)

right:
Shadow
1993
found fabric, thread, canvas
7 x 4.5in (18 x 12cm)
Collection of Sonya Clark and Darryl Harper

Shadow`, for instance, depicts a young child, bundled in a red parka and boots, arms outstretched to keep his balance on the tip of the much-too-small shadow he casts. It is embroidered on the threadbare knee of a child's blue corduroy pants, the fabric, like the shadow, just barely there. The colors, while not obviously trendy, nonetheless hark straight back to the 70s – those of us who were children then intuitively sense the subtle difference between the slightly muddied, polyester-infused reds, greens, and golds in Morris's remembered images of childhood and the tasteful pastels and crisp, cotton brights in which we dress our own children. Morris notes that his use of worn clothing also places the works – and their characters – within a social structure. Clothes usually reveal a gender, an economic class, a geographical or cultural region, often even an occupation and age in a person's life.

The physical structure that fabric and thread allow is also significant to these works. The structural effects in pieces like the aforementioned *Good Paper*, in which the father is built up with layers of fabric and thread, while the child is stitched in simple outline; or *In Bed*, in which a fully rendered figure lies despondently across a bed as a smaller, transparent figure gazes out the window, differentiated from the background only by the direction and density of the stitching; these would be impossible to achieve in any other medium.

above:

In Bed

2001

found fabric, sewing thread, canvas

7 x 7in (18 x 18cm)

right:

Pointing

2002

thread, canvas

4.8 x 6.3ft (1.5 x 2m)

Much has been made of the fact that Morris is a man who has chosen to sew, a pursuit our culture still considers primarily 'women's work.' While the art world – if not society at large – has moved away from associating gender too closely with media, the move is incomplete. Centuries of history that perceive embroidery as a feminine – and by extension inferior – art form provide an important subtext for this work, sharpening the bite of Morris's ongoing commentary on social inequities and lopsided power structures.

Recently, Morris has begun working on a much larger scale, making a shift from works as small as a snapshot to pieces approaching six or more feet. The new work is more linear, more monochromatic. Pieces such as *Pointing*, and *Who'll Be Sorry When Who's Gone?* (pp38, 40), are stitched in white thread on red and black canvas, respectively. While making embroideries on this scale invokes a complex set of technical issues (not to mention the time required to sew such a thing), it also brings the work into a very different psychological space for the viewer.

Looking at Morris's small-scale embroideries often has the psychological, if not visual, effect of looking through old snapshots. There is an element of nostalgia in them, although unlike most family albums they do not capture the celebrations and record the happy moments of the past. They tell a far more truthful tale, casting an unforgiving glare on the moments of fear and pain – the slap of rejection, the crush of broken promises and failed attempts to please. They may be snapshots of Morris's own exceptional past, but they invoke feelings that we all have experienced, and tend to choose to leave in the past.

Morris's most recent work tugs us into the present. Partly because of the scale – some of the figures approach life size – but also because of the transparency, the openness of the outlined images, and the sheer numbers of people depicted. In works such as *Pointing*, we are moved beyond the intimate circle of family or office, and into the public sphere. Viewing these images, we are nudged to be participants rather than mere observers. It is a challenging step, but one that holds satisfying rewards.

Ann Wiens
Painter, writer, editor
Chicago, USA

Color Plates

Target Practice
1995
craft felt, sewing thread, canvas
7 x 7in (18 x 18cm)

Baby Race
1988
thread, canvas
10 x 11in (26 x 28.5cm)

Playing Right Field
1990
found fabric, sewing thread, canvas
6.5 x 7in (17 x 18cm)

Untitled
1993
found fabric, sewing thread, canvas
7 x 10.5in (18 x 27cm)
Collection of Linda and Tom Dolack

Argument

2001

found fabric, sewing thread, canvas

6 x 9.5in (15.5 x 24.5cm)

You Promised Me
1993
found fabric, sewing thread, canvas
6 x 9in (15.5 x 23.5cm)
Collection of Linda and Tom Dolack

Fade
1995
found fabric, sewing thread, canvas
5 x 6in (13 x 15.5cm)

Turning Invisible
2002
sewing thread, canvas
4 x 4.5in (10.5 x 11.5cm)

Untitled
1994
collage, acrylic, ink, paper
9 x 10in (23.5 x 26cm)

Father and Son
1992
collage, acrylic, ink, paper
8 x 9in (21 x 23.5cm)

Company picnic
1997
found fabric, sewing thread, canvas
7 x 7in (18 x 18cm)
Collection of Lorraine and Harold Paddor

Embroidered text reads: NEVER USE GOOD PAPER TO DRAW ON! USE THE BACK OF A CALENDAR OR THE INSIDE OF AN ENVELOPE OF AN OLD

left:
Good Paper
2001
thread, canvas
8 x 6.5in (21 x 17cm)

right:
Climb (detail)
2002
thread, canvas
6.5 x 6.5ft (2 x 2m)

Lizzie
1994
cat hair, thread, canvas
6 x 5.5in (15.5 x 14.5cm)
Collection of Mary Bero

left:

Who'll Be Sorry When Who's Gone?
2001
thread, canvas
6 x 5ft (1.9 x 1.6m)

above:

Untitled
1992
thread, found vinyl, canvas
6.5 x 5in (17 x 13cm)

Who'll Be Sorry When Who's Gone? (detail)
2001
thread, canvas
6 x 5ft (1.9 x 1.6m)

Pointing (detail)
2002
thread, canvas
4.8 x 6.3ft (1.5 x 2m)

Biography

Born   1960, Barbourville, Kentucky

Education and Awards

2002   The ArtCouncil Award, Chicago

2000   Illinois Arts Council, Artists Fellowship Award

1990   Illinois Arts Council, Finalist Award

1987   MFA, The School of the Art Institute of Chicago

1985   BFA, University of Kentucky, Lexington

Current Position

                          Adjunct Associate Professor, The School of the Art Institute of Chicago

One and Two Person Exhibitions

2004   'Drawings' (1985 – 2004), gescheidle, Chicago

                          'Darrel Morris,' Lyons Wier Gallery, New York

1999   'Selected Cat Stories' (1986-1999), Lyons Wier Gallery, Chicago

1997   'Busted Flat,' Lyons Wier Gallery, Chicago

                          'Tom Lundberg and Darrel Morris,' Jan Weiner Gallery, Kansas City, Missouri

1996   'Housework,' Wood Street Gallery, Chicago

                          'Telling Objects,' University of Southern Maine, Gorham, Maine

1995   'Darrel Morris,' Lyons Wier & Ginsberg Gallery, Chicago

1990   'David Mann, Darrel Morris,' Dart Gallery, Chicago

1989   'Darrel Morris and Elena Corsi,' Missouri Gallery, Chicago

1987   'Darrel Morris and David Kwan,' The School of the Art Institute, Superior St. Gallery, Chicago

South East Essex College
of Ar... ...end

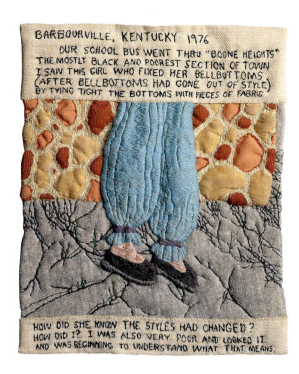

Embroidered text on artwork:

BARBOURVILLE, KENTUCKY 1976
OUR SCHOOL BUS WENT THRU "BOONE HEIGHTS"
THE MOSTLY BLACK AND POOREST SECTION OF TOWN
I SAW THIS GIRL WHO FIXED HER BELLBOTTOMS
(AFTER BELLBOTTOMS HAD GONE OUT OF STYLE)
BY TYING TIGHT THE BOTTOMS WITH PIECES OF FABRIC

HOW DID SHE KNOW THE STYLES HAD CHANGED?
HOW DID I? I WAS ALSO VERY POOR AND LOOKED IT
AND WAS BEGINNING TO UNDERSTAND WHAT THAT MEANS.

Bellbottoms

2001

found fabric, sewing thread, canvas

6.5 x 6in (17 x 15.5cm)

Collection of Stephen Pratt

Selected Group Exhibitions

2003	'Embroidery in the 21st Century,' Delaware Center for the Contemporary Arts, Wilmington, Delaware
	Group show, John Michael Kohler Arts Center, Sheboygan, Wisconsin
2002	'Here and Now,' Chicago Cultural Center, Chicago
	'Hobby Lobby,' Gallery 312, Chicago
	'Grief Mopping,' Neutral Ground Gallery, Regina, Saskatchewan, Canada
2001	'Tell Me a Story,' Cahoon Museum of American Art, Cotuit, Massachusetts
	'Small Pleasures,' Lyons Wier Gallery, Chicago
2000	'Remnants of Memory,' Asheville Art Museum, Asheville, North Carolina
	'Heritage, Salvaged, Embroidered.' Marylhurst University, Marylhurst, Oregon
1999	'Count Down…,' Bucheon Gallery, San Francisco
	'Men of the Cloth,' Loveland Museum, Loveland, Colorado (tour)
1998	'Small World,' The Museum for Textiles, Toronto, Ontario, Canada
	'Image & Object,' The Sybaris Gallery, Royal Oak, Michigan
1997	'Stitchers and Beaders; America's Best,' Ohio Craft Museum, Columbus, Ohio
1995	'Conceptual Textiles,' John Michael Kohler Arts Center, Sheboygan, Wisconsin

continued

1994	'Fifty-fifth Anniversary,' Hyde Park Art Center, Chicago.
1993	'Material Departures,' Illinois Art Gallery, Chicago
	'When Push Comes to Shove,' Randolph Street Gallery, Chicago
1992	'Telling Stories,' Loyola Art Gallery, Loyola University, Chicago
	'Celebrating the Stitch,' Newton Arts Center, St. Paul, Minnesota (tour)
1991	'Louder,' Gallery 400, Chicago
	'It Figures,' University of Wisconsin - Eau Claire, Wisconsin
1990	'Sinister: Sinister Art and the Art of the Sinister,' N.A.M.E. Gallery, Chicago
	'Fiber: United States/ Colombia,' Tallahassee, FL and Bogota, Columbia (tour)
1989	'Chicago works: Art from the Windy City,' Bruce Gallery, Edinboro, Pennsylvania
1988	'Young Americans,' American Craft Museum, New York
	The School of the Art Institute/ Centro Colombia Americano:
	Traveling Exhibition, Medelin, Columbia

Selected Publications and Reviews

2003	*Mouthtomouth*, spring, Interview by Julie Farstad.
	Chicago Social, May, 'We are Living in a Material World,' essay by Ann Wiens.
2002	*Chicago Tribune*, December 1, 'Artist Weaves Life into Fabric,' essay by Lisa Stein.
2001	*New Art Examiner*, May, review by Jean Robertson.
2000	*The New York Times*, November 21, review by William Zimmer.
1998	*Surface Design Journal*, spring, 'The Masculine in Fiber,' essay by Mark Newport.
	'Small World,' catalog essay by Sarah Quinton.
1995	'Conceptual Textiles,' catalog essay by Alison Ferris.
	New Art Examiner, November, review by Polly Ullrich.
	Chicago Magazine, November, 'Needles and Pains,' essay by Ann Wiens.
1994	*Fiberarts*, summer, 'A Plea for Broader Dialogue,' essay by Anne Wilson.
1993	*Fiberarts*, November/ December, 'Fiber Close to Home,' essay by Margo Mensing.
1992	*Arts Magazine*, February, 'Home Economics,' essay by Maureen P. Sherlock.
1991	*Metropolis*, July/ August, 'The Threads of Modern Life,' essay by Ann Batchelder.
	Celebrating the Stitch, The Taunton Press, Newton, Connecticut, author Barbara Lee Smith.
1990	*Arts Magazine*, October, review by Kathryn Hixson.

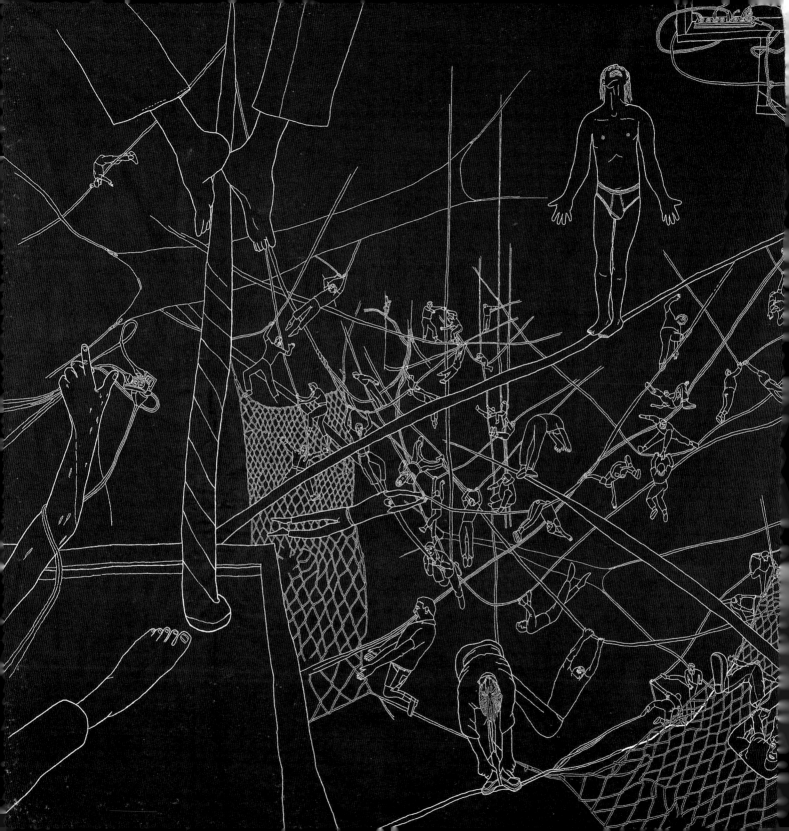